# HEARTS TOUCHING
*Love Letters from a Poet*

VOLUME 2

# HEARTS TOUCHING

*Love Letters from a Poet*

# BILL WEBER

Copyrighted Material

Hearts Touching: Love Letters From A Poet
Copyright © 2017 by Bill Weber.
All Rights Reserved.

No part of this publication may be reproduced, stored
in a retrieval system or transmitted, in any form or by any
means–electronic, mechanical, photocopying, recording or
otherwise–without prior written permission from
the publisher, except for the inclusion of brief
quotations in a review.

For information about this title or to order other books and/
or electronic media, contact the publisher:
Quality Choices
2607 Zent Drive
Vandalia, Illinois 62471
www.BillWeberAuthor.com

ISBNs:
978-0-9971317-1-0 (hardcover)
978-0-9971317-2-7 (softcover)
978-0-9971317-5-8 (eBook)

Printed in the United States of America

Cover and Interior design: 1106 Design

This is dedicated to every woman,

to every woman who has ever thought she wasn't attractive enough,

to every woman who hasn't fully experience the beauty of her femininity,

to every woman who has ever minimized any aspect of her personal beauty as a woman,

to every woman who has ever doubted that she deserves to touch and be touched very sensuously,

to every woman who was afraid to be fully present in her body fully making love,

to every woman who has ever yearned to embrace the depths of passion inherent in her being as a woman,

to every woman who doesn't love being in her body right now.

This is dedicated to everyone who has yet to realize,

that there is someone out there for everyone including you,

that you are not the only one looking, someone is looking for you as much as you are looking for them, someone is dreaming of being with you, just as much as you are dreaming of being with them,

they are often found in the most-unlikeliest of places,

and they are often much, much closer than you think.

And this is dedicated to every man who deeply wants a woman's love and has no clue where to even begin to find the words a woman needs to hear.

# Contents

| | | |
|---|---|---|
| Introduction | | ix |
| How To Read This Book | | xvii |
| 1 | Your Fragrance | 2 |
| | Sweetens With Age | 5 |
| | Want Me | 7 |
| 2 | Into Sensuous Suede | 10 |
| | Imagining You | 13 |
| | Hearts Touching | 15 |
| 3 | Take My Hand | 19 |
| | Intoxication Of Sensation | 20 |
| | Sweetness Of Caress | 23 |
| 4 | Of Cotton Sheets | 26 |
| | Afterglow | 29 |
| | Within Your Kiss | 31 |

| | | |
|---|---|---|
| 5 | To Be Caressed | 34 |
| | Overwhelm My Senses | 36 |
| | Heaven's Kiss | 38 |
| 6 | Single Field Of Love | 43 |
| | Carry Me | 45 |
| | Masculinity Surrendering | 47 |
| 7 | Sweet Pleasures | 51 |
| | Dancing Slow | 52 |
| | In Your Heart | 55 |
| 8 | Nectar Of Femininity | 59 |
| | To Be Desired | 60 |
| | Desired By You | 62 |
| 9 | Ecstasy Of Love | 66 |
| | In Your Bliss | 69 |
| | Angelic Lips | 70 |
| Acknowledgments | | 73 |
| Contributing Photographers | | 75 |
| About The Author | | 79 |
| Other Publications By Bill Weber | | 81 |

# Introduction

## *Spiritual Beings*

We are not spiritual beings trapped in physical bodies. Our spiritual nature and our physical form are two sides of the same leaf growing on the tree of life. We are petals of a single flower, flowers on the same stem rooted in the same soil across endless fields blossoming with the seamless energy of a single sun.

We are interlocking facets of a single crystal, interconnected patterns emerging from within a crystalline universe. We are every tiny feather, in unison, empowering the wings of every bird lifting miraculously into flight. We are consciousness waking up, consciousness viewing itself from multitudes of varied perspectives, consciousness becoming aware of itself.

Everything in the universe is energy, including our physical body. It is the nature of our senses to interpret these energy patterns and translate them into perceptions that our thinking mind can understand. It is this translation that creates for us the illusion of solidity and the illusion of duality or separateness. The seeming solidity of the world of separate individual forms is a perceptual illusion of our senses.

## *Presence*

Being spiritual, being present, and self-realization are different ways of talking about the same thing. Our spiritual nature, our connection with the Divine order of the universe, is not something we must seek. It is not lost and does not need to be found. It can never be damaged, broken or cut off from us - because it *is* us. It flourishes eternally within us and through us whether we believe in it or consciously perceive it or not. It is without judgment. It is without past or future. There is nothing to do first, nothing to overcome, nothing to learn or achieve in-order-to get there, because there is no "there" to get to. It is always here, now, in this present moment, in you, because there is only one eternal present moment. And it is always now. This is presence.

*Introduction*

The only time we are not aware of our spiritual nature is when our mind is distracting us from the fullness of the present moment, the fullness of life in this and every present moment. Our mind constantly tells us stories. Our mind tells us stories about other times and other places. In other words, we are in our head rather than in our body. When we are living and reliving the stories in our head we are not fully experiencing life in and around our body in this present moment. For most people on the planet this is almost continuous.

## *Awareness*

Awareness of our inner body, attention to our breathing, immersing ourselves in sensations and movement is presence. Every moment that we shift our awareness into our body we experience the spiritual nature of being.

The deeper we allow ourselves to feel and experience our breathing, the movement of our body, and the aliveness of our physical sensations, the more fully alive and present we are right now. And the freer we are from the stories in our head.

Our lives are typically filled with so much thinking about other places and other times, past or future, that the true consciousness of our being is perpetually obscured. It is like being lost in a mental dream, lost in time consciousness where everything seems to have a past and a future. While in time consciousness our mind is continually reacting to stories of the past and trying to control stories of the future. When the present is experienced as, something you have to go through to get to something in the future, the present is reduced to nothing more than a means to an end.

## *Sensations*

Sensations are a very powerful portal bringing our awareness back into our body. The more awareness we have in our body, the less dialogue we have in our head. When we pay attention to sensations in our body there is less available for the mind to preoccupy us with past and future. Sensations take us out of our head and bring us back into our body, out of time consciousness into space consciousness. This is the simplicity of presence.

*Introduction*

This is the reason people crave experiences like sky diving, racing, mountain climbing and other extreme sports. During these experiences we are so intensely alive in the experience that there is no room left over for the voice in the head. It's gone. And it feels so good to be fully alive in the present moment of life without the distraction of the voice in our head because this is our true nature.

Our body is a temple and consciously dwelling in our temple is a sacred practice. Any activity that gets us out of our head and into our body can be a sacred practice. Any activity into which we lose ourselves, we become submerged in, we get in the zone, can be a sacred practice. It might be singing, gardening, dancing, baking, painting, etc.

The more submersed we are in sensations, the more conscious we are of the only thing that is real, the only thing there ever is, this present moment. This is sacred.

## *Sex*

The reason we crave sex is not just because it feels so good. The intimacy of the connection quiets the voice in our head. The intensity of the sensations pulls us out of our head and into our body. It takes us out of time consciousness into space consciousness.

When you make love, you touch and love another human being in the most intimate and personal ways. You disrobe, expose and share your body with another human being who also disrobes, exposes and shares their body with you. You allow yourself to become vulnerable, to give and to receive in the most personal ways. And this is only the beginning.

## *Making Love as a Spiritual Practice*

Every time we make love is another opportunity to recognize how the spiritual principles of Yin and Yang represent themselves through the design of our bodies and the pleasures of the experience. It is another opportunity to experience the joy of transcending the illusion of duality, and another step along the spiritual journey of awakening to the true nature of our being.

Making love is a physical expression of the interplay of Yin and Yang energy, a joyous celebration of the human body, a sensual fountain of pleasures, a regenerating

*Introduction*

process of sacred energetic potential, and a hint of the joy of the heaven of enlightenment.

Savor the sacredness of the being you are with. Savor the intimacy of the connection. Savor the ebb and flow of energy. Savor every sensation. Savor the sacredness of every little thing in life.

# How To Read This Book

Read every word
Pause on every line
Believe every image

See every curve
Feel every texture
Appreciate every sensation

Enjoy every thought
Step into every concept
Love every feeling

Savor every aroma
Taste every drop
Experience every embrace

Live every moment

Become everything

Embrace life fully

*Part 1*

Your Fragrance
Sweetens With Age
Want Me

## Your Fragrance

    Your fragrance in the air
    Envelopes my consciousness

    Your face close to mine
    Takes my breath away

    Your voice in my ear
    Sings angelic chants

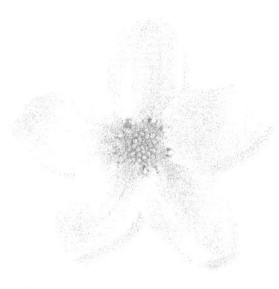

Your cheek against mine
Soothes my racing mind

Your lips on my neck
Raises goose bumps

Your fingers on my skin
Sends tingles down my spine

Your body against mine
Dissolves time and space

Your arms around my waist
Brings the universe into my heart

Your softness against my lips
Carries me into bliss

Your femininity intoxicates

## Hearts Touching

# Sweetens With Age

The allure of a woman deepens with age
The gentle invitation in her eyes
The depth of passion in her heart
The sweetness of femininity in her being

A woman's beauty grows with age
The touch of her hands
The caress of her skin
The smile on her lips

A woman's body sweetens with age
The seductive kiss of her lips
The tingle of her tongue loving yours
The intoxicating aroma of her arousal

The appeal of a woman multiplies with age
The softness of her breasts against your cheeks
The texture of her nipples between your lips
The warmth of her thighs around your body

## Hearts Touching

## Want Me

Eyes meet from across the room
Breath stops
Heart pounds

Imagination races
Throat gulps
Knees buckle

Peripheral vision fades
Time stops
Heart longs

Could you want me?
Could you choose me?
Could you take me to heaven?

*Part 2*

Into Sensuous Suede
Imagining You
Hearts Touching

*Hearts Touching*

# INTO SENSUOUS SUEDE

A woman ages like the sweetness of grapes
    fermenting into fine wine
A woman ages like spring flowers preceding the
    lush green fullness of summer

A woman ages like the magic of raw minerals
    transmuting into glistening gems
A woman ages like the fading colors of sunset
    gracefully revealing the infinite sparkling stars
    of the night sky

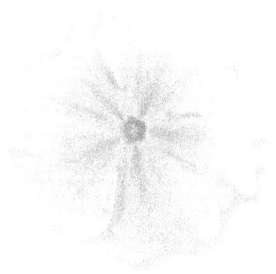

A woman ages like fresh milk curing into rich
   creamy cheese
A woman ages like milled flour rising into warm
   soft bread with honey butter

A woman ages like brushing smooth leather into
   soft sensuous swede
A woman ages like gradually uncovering a breath-
   taking masterpiece, one item of clothing
   at a time

A woman aging is the multiplying of levels of
   what beauty means
A woman aging is the spiritual nature of the
   universe revealing its mysteries of sacred
   pleasures

## Hearts Touching

# Imagining You

When your lips move
Gracefully sleek
Rhythmically balanced

Words fade into background
Coherency tries to focus
But I can no longer speak

Sounds become musical accompaniment
Vision melts into sensations of you
Quivering with need to connect

Imagining all of me in your sweet caress
Captivating all my senses
My heart is yours for the taking

# Hearts Touching

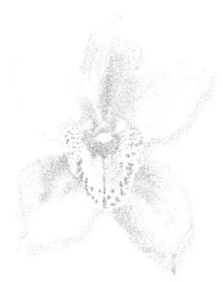

# Hearts Touching

Milk chocolate melting in your mouth
Whipped cream between your lips
Mint julep on your tongue
Cherry on top

Down comforter
Satin sheets
Warm skin
Sensual delight

Candlelight flickering
Silhouettes dancing
Moonlight bathing
After glowing

Hands holding hands
Lips kissing lips
Skin caressing skin
Hearts touching hearts

*Part 3*

Take My Hand
Intoxication Of Sensation
Sweetness Of Caress

*Hearts Touching*

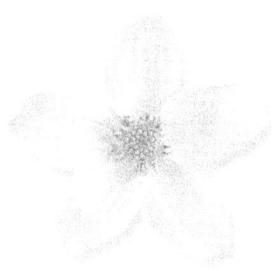

## Take My Hand

Looking into the depths of your eyes
Longing for your passions alive in my arms
The sweetness of your caress
The taste of your lips

Even from a distance you intoxicate me
The closer you get the harder my heart pounds
The rise and fall of your breasts as you breathe
Thinking of nothing but your touch

Struggling for the courage to show you a sign
The inadequacy of words to express
The pounding of my heart like thunder
Hoping you would take my hand and . . .

## INTOXICATION OF SENSATION

Every woman's caress is the living warmth
    of the sun
the softness of clouds
the splendor of sunrise

Every woman's kiss is the living endorphins
    of chocolate
the sweetness of honey
the bubbles of Moscato

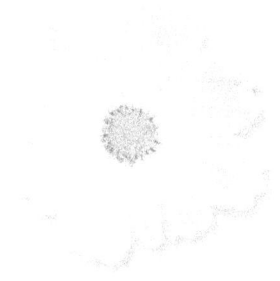

Every woman's love is the living essence of rose
the fragrance of jasmine
the intoxication of sensation

Every woman's body is the most precious
    of all gems
the most desirable of all gifts
the most sacred of all temples

You are the culmination of perfection
the pleasures of heaven
the fulfillment of my passion

## Hearts Touching

## Sweetness Of Caress

They are living emissaries of heaven
They are living metaphors of femininity
They are living demonstrations of perfection

They are the joy of life
They are the softness of love
They are the sweetness of caress

They are ageless in their allure
They are irresistible in their seduction
They are perfection in their form, as they are,
 right now

They intoxicate consciousness with their presence
They overwhelm senses with their touch
They tantalize lips with their response

Their energy grows in femininity with every year
Their passion to satisfy intensifies with every caress
Their sensitivity to love blossoms with every kiss

# *Part 4*

Of Cotton Sheets
Afterglow
Within Your Kiss

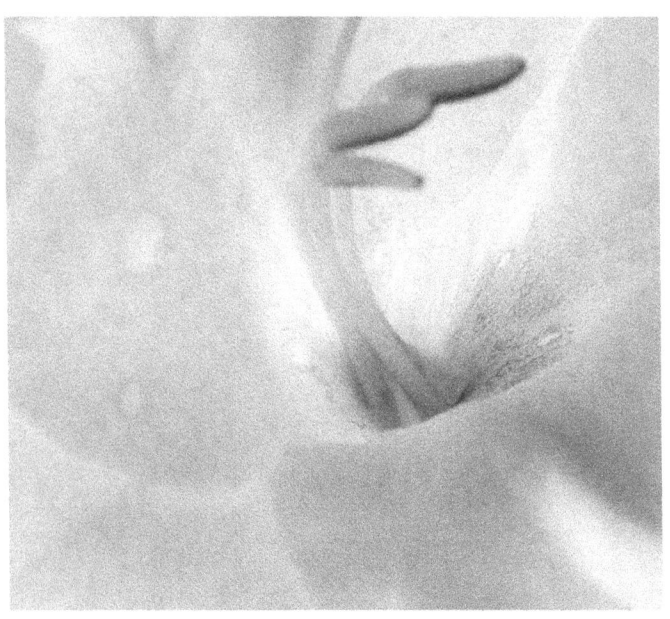

## OF COTTON SHEETS

He is the gentleness of trees rising to touch her
She is the vastness of the sky

He is the earth bathed in her love
She is the warmth of sunlight

He is a seed
She is fertility

She is the softness of cotton sheets
He is the firmness of steady support

She is the expression of angels entering his heart
He is the power of love igniting her passion

She is the embodiment of heaven
He is the physical form entering the gates

He offers himself to fulfill
She opens herself to receive

He enters the center of her being
She envelops him

He releases himself to her
She absorbs him

She is his feminine nature bringing him back to balance
He is her masculine nature releasing her femininity

She is him reflecting his yin
He is her reflecting her yang

They are one as they live in experience together

## Hearts Touching

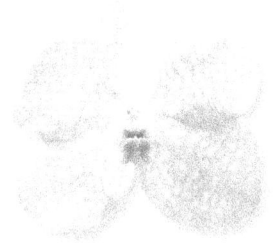

## Afterglow

Silk pajamas
Satin sheets
Sliding into position
Slipping into place

Gentle fingers
Genuine feelings
Filling your body
Fulfilling your soul

Down pillows
Down under
Gratifying our senses
Glorifying our love

Warm skin
Nestled spoons
Candle glow showing
Afterglow growing

## Hearts Touching

# Within Your Kiss

The sweetness of your attention disarms me
The pureness of your femininity absorbs me
The sensuousness of your lips envelops me with love

All words, all thinking erased by your power
All of my body, all of me, within your kiss
All masculinity surrendered into your love

Surrendered into pureness of femininity
Surrendered into magical sensations of angelic lips
Surrendered into heavenly fulfillment of love

Yang flows forth into the heart of yin
Yin fulfills the soul of yang with her kiss
Physical duality becomes as one in love

*Part 5*

To Be Caressed
Overwhelm My Senses
Heaven's Kiss

# TO BE CARESSED

>They are here to show us the softness of
>>every woman
>to soften our gaze and soften our hearts
>
>They are here before us to be noticed
>to attract attention and to feel attractive

They are here to comfort and be comforted
to cuddle and be cuddled

They are here to appreciate and be appreciated
to cherish and be cherished

They are here to love and be loved
to hold and be held

They are here to caress and be caressed
to give pleasure and receive pleasure

They are here to tantalize and be tantalized
To kiss and be kissed

They are here to draw us into our bodies
to tingle with the ecstasy of touch

They are here to teach us to live in the present
to demonstrate how life is heaven on earth

## OVERWHELM MY SENSES

Just being in the same room with you
    overwhelms my senses
The sound of your voice carries me away
The movement of your body hypnotizes
Every gesture draws in all awareness

Imagining the smoothness of your skin on my cheek
The aliveness of your body in my arms
The thrill of your hands touching me
Every breath you take pumps warm blood
    through my body

Dreaming that you could want me the way I
    want you
The depth of color in your eyes seeing me
The smoothness of each strand of hair between
    my fingers
Every glance of your eyes stops time

Struggling for the courage to show you a sign
The inadequacy of words to express
The pounding of my heart like thunder
And yet unable to speak or move

Longing for your passions alive in my arms
The taste of your lips
The sweetness of your caress
Hoping you could see my heart and . . .

# Heaven's Kiss

Totally vulnerable to your choice
Totally surrendered to your will
Totally succumbed to your angelic kiss

Myself being chosen by this angel's love
My heart feeling the overwhelming joy of being
 so wanted
My sacred angel sensuously coaxing the essence
 of my soul to her

All muscles relax into the power of your femininity
Time and space dissolve into the softness of your
 femininity
Masculine form releases into the sweetness
 of your femininity

Kissing the depths of my soul with your impassioned
 sensations
Fulfilling the depths of my heart through
 the sweetness of your love
Ingesting the depths of me into the beauty
 of your being

*Part 6*

Single Field Of Love
Carry Me
Masculinity Surrendering

## Hearts Touching

## Single Field Of Love

Hands supporting the back of my head
Holding my face to the sweetness of heaven
Held and comforted in angelic arms

Masculine and feminine dovetailing back to balance
Magical sensations of your softness absorb me
My consciousness glows from within
    your beating heart

Completely melting into your body as one
Consciousness experiencing the reality
    of our oneness
Combined fields of sensation realizing they are
    a single field of love

## Hearts Touching

## Carry Me

You know just how, where and what to do
Each movement like a new beginning
As if you know my mind and feel my feelings

You melt me into lovingness with your touch
Every sensation building from the last
As if you know just where and how to take
    me further

You carry me all the way to the peaks of heaven
All consciousness blending into your sweet caress
As if you know my very soul and kiss me there

## Hearts Touching

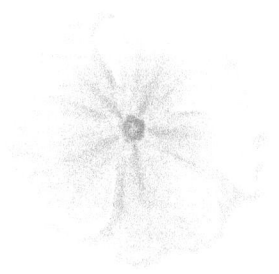

# Masculinity Surrendering

Filled with the sweetness of your love
Succumbed to your angelic femininity
Compelled by your gentle advancement

Time fades away with your kiss
Muscles relax into your softness
Masculine form becomes one with your energy

Femininity coaxing the essence of masculinity into
    your physical form
Masculinity surrendering its essence to your love
Humanity merging into the spiritual oneness
    that we are

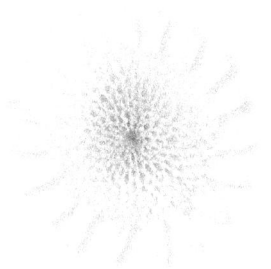

*Part 7*

Sweet Pleasures
Dancing Slow
In Your Heart

## Hearts Touching

# Sweet Pleasures

Volcano muffins
Hot totties
Whipped cream

Fingers in the honey pot
Lips around the candy cane
Frosting on your tongue

Savory aroma wafting
Cream filling bursting
Sweet pleasures gratifying

Melting marshmallows
Warm gooey cookies
Soft butter melting on your buns

You are my comfort food

*Hearts Touching*

# Dancing Slow

She longed to snuggle a lover in bed
She longed to touch and please
She longed to respond to every pleasure
She longed to satisfy his every desire

She thought she might never be touched again
She thought she might never be cuddled
She thought that no one could ever want her body
She thought that no one even looked

She believed her beauty had faded
She believed her skin had sagged
She believed her body was flawed
She believed her days of love had passed her by

He dreamed of kissing her hand in the moonlight
He dreamed of touching her skin with his cheek
He dreamed of dancing slow in her arms
He dreamed of waking in the morning by her side

He imagined caressing every inch of her body
He imagined pleasing her every response
He imagined responding to her every desire
He imagined loving her all night long

He was sure he had no chance with her
He was sure she would never respond
He was sure he could never be so lucky
He was sure he would lose if he tried

## Hearts Touching

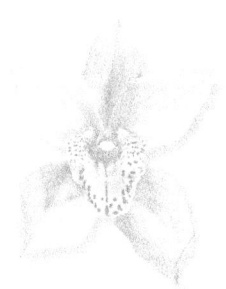

# In Your Heart

Caress me to heaven with angelic lips
Absorb me with your sensuous kiss
Love me until my inner soul comes forth

Desire all of me to release to you
Take all of my essence into your heart
Accept every drop of me with your love

Encourage all of me to release to you
Accept all of me into your being
Desire every drop of me with your love

I hear my living essence beating in your heart
I see my glowing essence alive within your heart
I feel my sacred essence cherished throughout
    every part

*Part 8*

Nectar Of Femininity
To Be Desired
Desired By You

## Hearts Touching

# Nectar Of Femininity

Fully loving your deepest femininity
Allowed into the most sacred of all places
Allowed to partake in this secret touch

Losing track of separation
Not sure where you begin and where I end
Right here, right now is our universe

Melting ever deeper into your impassioned responses
Receiving the taste of your sacred nourishment
Ageless timeless nectar of femininity

Chosen by you to be here now
Allowed to release your angelic passions
With this most intimate kiss of love

# To Be Desired

They are the quintessential symbols of femininity
They are emissaries of heaven

They are living joy
They are every woman's body

They are here before us to be noticed
attract attention and enjoy their allure

They are here to touch and be touched
to enthrall and respond

They are here to desire and be desired
to nuzzle and be nuzzled

They are here to adore and be adored
to cherish and be cherished

They are here to bring joy and experience joy
to nourish our souls and be nourished by caress

They are here to tantalize and be tantalized
to tingle with the ecstasy of being loved

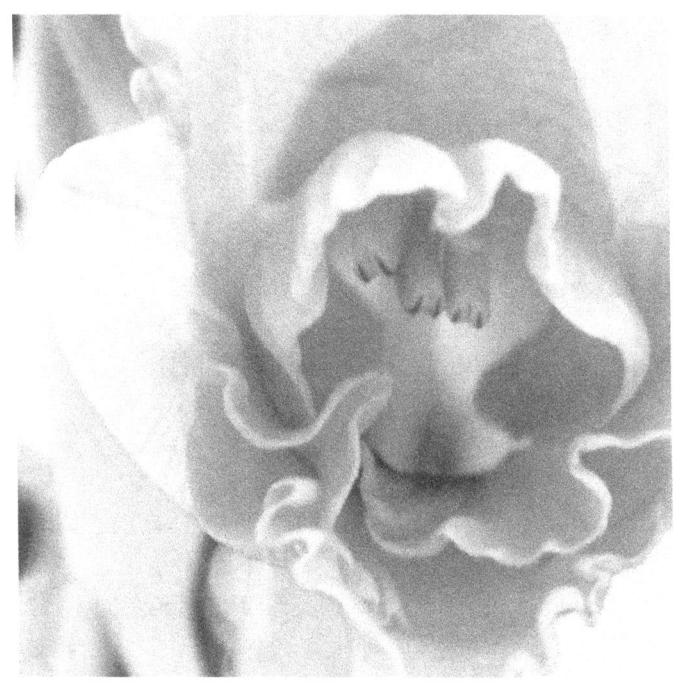

## Desired By You

> Inner self prays
> Inner heart hopes
> Deepest being seeks your touch
> Deepest essence yearns for your kiss

Thrilled by such personal caress
Thrilled by such personal attention
Sensuousness of your personal caress
Sensuousness of your personal kiss

So deeply desired
So completely accepted
All of me desired by your love
All of me accepted by your kiss

My deepest feelings so vulnerable
My deepest essence so accepted
Essence of my manhood so desired by you
Essence of my manhood so completely released
    by the femininity of your kiss

*Part 9*

Ecstasy Of Love
In Your Bliss
Angelic Lips

# Ecstasy Of Love

Warm water running
Soaped up skin
Lips tasting lips

Bodies uniting
Love connecting
Tenderness fulfilling

Smooth textures
Slippery curves
Sliding hands

Comfort of togetherness
Clarity of aliveness
Completion of oneness

Tingling hearts
Touching fingers
Thrilling sensations

Intimacy of the universe
Closeness of being
Ecstasy of love

## Hearts Touching

# In Your Bliss

Opening to me
Encouraging my caress
Responding to my touch

Moving gently to accommodate more love
Allowing me into more sweetly intimate places
Leading my fingers to the gates of heaven

You are the yin balancing my yang
You are my heaven in the palm of my hand
You are the perfection of a universal plan

Loving you with sacred kiss
My turn for you to feel my deepest love
Your turn for me to revel in your bliss

# Angelic Lips

Completely vulnerable to you
Completely surrendered to you
Completely safe within your love

Sweetness of your lips surrounds my being
Sweetness of your lips draws all of me to you
Sweetness of your lips absorbs my consciousness

The angel within you wants my response
The angel within you brings your lips to me
The angel within you takes me to heaven

All of me within the warm smoothness of angelic
    lips
All of me magically caressed by the sweetness of
    your attention
All of me feeling loved and wanted by the woman
    I crave

The woman I crave wanting to experience all of
    me in this most personal way
The woman I crave reaching into the depths of
    my soul to want me the way I want her
The woman I crave wanting me to release the
    very essence of my being to her in this sacred
    connection of love

# Acknowledgments

Special Advisor, Consultant and Coach:
Cynthia S. Becker

Editorial and Technical Support:
Michele DeFilippo and Ronda Rawlins at 1106 Design

Additional Advice and Support:
Joan Hurd at Hurd & Associates Design

## Contributing Photographers

The following photographers generously donated their photos and courageously agreed to allow me to alter, modify, Photoshop and overlay their photos in any way I chose to create these and future beautiful presentations for you.

Christine Wuertz: Photographer, Christine Wuertz® is a photographer/graphic designer from the St. Louis, Missouri area. She works as a designer and screen printer.

Eileen Witte: Photographer, Eileen Witte, is someone who is very drawn to flowers and on occasion sees something, a flower, a grouping of flowers, a magnificent sunset, a butterfly, an abstract, that she wants to keep, so she takes a picture of it, and like all things she puts her heart into they turn out amazing.

Carol Madding: Photographer and Actress, Carol Madding, resides in Mariposa, California, on the border of the Sierra National Forest, and creates beautiful photographs of all kinds that capture the beauty and emotional character of her subject matter. Having fun with her photos, she has created wonderful memory books for young children. In addition to photography she is an accomplished actor in movies and commercials, published singer, writer, and grandmother.

Carmel Beth Kemmerling: Photographer, was born and raised in Southern Connecticut and ventured to the Midwest to attend Tarkio College, receiving a BA in Biology/Psychology. She fell in love with the midwestern atmosphere and small town charm and continues to reside there. She works as a Business Office Manager at a Long Term Facility in NW Missouri. In her free time enjoys her artistry capturing flowers, scenery and people through the eye of her camera.

*Contributing Photographers*

Gibb: Photographer, Gibb, lives in Colorado and enjoys gardening and cooking for friends.

Tiger Lily Flower Shop: A special thanks to all the women at Tiger Lily in Vandalia, Illinois for so generously allowing me to take pictures of their outstandingly beautiful flowers.

## About The Author

Bill has been called a time traveler. He was sent here from our future where the unique beauty and attractiveness of every individual is apparent. He was sent here to open a window into a time and place where everyone feels good enough right now, a time where we honor, respect and cherish the sacredness of every human being, a place where no one has time to make war because everyone would rather make love.

# Other Publications by Bill Weber

## *Books:*

Choosing Me, Love Letters from a Poet, Volume 1, by Bill Weber

Hearts Touching, Love Letters from a Poet, Volume 2, by Bill Weber

*www.BillWeberAuthor.com*

## *Audio Recordings:*

Get Sleep Healing, Full Night Sleep Version, (Formerly known as 'Accelerated Healing' Night time Version), by Bill Weber & Cynthia S. Becker

Get Sleep Healing, Refreshing Nap Version, (Formerly known as 'Accelerated Healing' Daytime Version), by Bill Weber & Cynthia S. Becker

*www.GetSleepHealing.com*

www.ingramcontent.com/pod-product-compliance
Lightning Source LLC
Chambersburg PA
CBHW052105070526
44584CB00017B/2347